This Journal Belongs To:

Copyright 2020 Author Talk Media, LLC

All rights reserved. In accordance of the U.S. Copyright Act of 1975, no part of this publication may be reproduced, distributed, or transmitted in any form or by any means, including photocopying, recording, or other electronic or mechanical methods, without the prior written permission of the publisher, except in the case of brief quotations embodied in critical reviews and certain other noncommercial uses permitted by copyright law.

This is a work of fiction. Names, characters, places, and incidents either are the products of the author's imagination or are used fictitiously. Any resemblance to actual persons, living or dead, businesses, companies, events, or locales is entirely coincidental.

FBI Anti-Piracy Warning: The unauthorized reproduction or distribution of a copyrighted work is illegal. Criminal copyright infringement, including infringement without monetary gain, is investigated by the FBI and is punishable by fines and federal imprisonment. The unauthorized reproduction or distribution of a copyrighted work is illegal. Criminal copyright infringement is investigated by federal law enforcement agencies and is punishable by up to five years in prison and a fine of $250,000.

Cover Created by Naomi Lane

Cover Image: Shutterstock

Lined Journal designed by artsbynaty

ABOUT GENA SHOWALTER

Gena Showalter is the *New York Times* and *USA TODAY* bestselling author of a crapton of books. Seriously! She's written 100 brand new stories – well, almost. Everything from paranormal, fantasy, sci-fi and contemporary romance, to young adult fairy tales.

She's also written a non-fiction how to guide about writing your own novel, co-authored with best friend/business partner/fellow author and journal enthusiast, Jill Monroe. Some of Showalter's tales are sexy, some are sweet, but whatever you're in the mood for, she's got you covered. She's currently claimed by 2 cats and 7 dogs, but it's not weird because she's a rescue. Oh, yes, and she has 2 kids, too, but they are both adults.

When she isn't hard at work planning or writing her next novel, she's been known to morph into the most boring person in the world. We said what we said.

GenaShowalter.com

I am passionate about journals! Every time I start writing a new book, I select a new journal to help me keep track of story thoughts, ideas for future scenes, plot, characters and sometimes I'll even write entire chapters longhand.

Maybe you dream of writing your own book. Maybe you want to keep notes about life or love as you go about your day.

Let my Lords of the Underworld guide you along the way. These immortal demon possessed warriors are thrilled to offer a fresh piece of advice on every page. Oh, a word of advice from me—you're probably going to need bail money.

All my best,

Gena Showalter

> Being kind is always free.
> So be cruel and make everyone pay.
> —William the Ever Randy

/ /

> Always consider the foes
> and the cons.
>
> —Torin, Keeper of Disease

/ /

> Never backstab!
> Okay, sometimes backstab. Fine!
> Always backstab AND front stab.
> Stab from every angle to be sure.
>
> —Keeley, the Red Queen

/ /

> Don't regret tomorrow! Consider the chaos and destruction you could cause today.
>
> —Anya, major goddess of anarchy, keeping it klassy

/ /

> You don't need a reason.
> You just need an excuse...
> —Sunny, Killer Unicorn Shifter

/   /

> A hero is only as good as the villain standing behind him with a blade.
> —Hades, Exalted King of All Hells

/ /

> Keep them on pins and needles. If that doesn't work, keep them on spikes. Forget messy. Get results.
>
> —Maddox, Keeper of Violence

/   /

> Find a significant other who is 90% monster, 10% cuddle bear.
>
> —Ashlyn Lord,
> Mother of the Sweetest of Demons

/ /

> If it only bleeds a little, you're doing it wrong.
>
> —Danika Lord, Dagger Aficionado

/ /

> Just because the first wound hurts, doesn't mean you won't enjoy the second.
>
> —Reyes Lord, Master of Pain

/ /

> Scars are like catnip.
> Get one, and you'll get some.
> —Lucien Lord, Keeper of Death

> When in doubt, pout!
>
> —Paris Lord,
> Keeper of Promiscuity

> Yes, you SHOULD overreact.
>
> —Sienna Lord, Keeper of Wrath

> Where there's a will,
> there's a possible inheritance!
>
> —Rathbone, King of Your Mother

/ /

> The best tattoos
> are the worst tattoos.
> I said what I said.
>
> —Amun Lord, the Vault

> You don't HAVE to cause chaos.
> You GET to.
> —Haidee Lord, Love Guru

/ /

> What are you waiting for? Send it. They WANT to see your junk.
> —Strider Lord, Keeper of Defeat

/ /

> Change is for quitters.
> And stuffing into bags to beat the bad guys.
>
> —Kaia the Wing Shredder

/ /

> The more enemies you acquire, the more reasons you have to lash out. Win/win.
>
> —Gwen Lord, Half Harpy, Half Demon, All Warrior

/ /

> If you've got it, taunt it.
>
> —Bianka,
> Mistress of Wicked Delights

/ /

> Yes, you should comment.
> They'll love you for it.
>
> —Lysander,
> Official Wrangler of Bianka

> Yes, yes.
> Stroke your hate like a lover.
> —Sabin Lord, Keeper of Doubts

/ /

> Yes, but are you monstrous **ENOUGH?**
>
> —Galen, Keeper of Jealousy and False Hope

/ /

> Always jump to conclusions.
> It saves time.
>
> —Fox, Keeper of Distrust

/   /

> Don't get even.
> Get more vengeance.
> —Legion Honey Lord

/ /

> Their every tear is a tiny reward for a job well done.
> —Aeron Lord

/ /

> Why text when you could call at 2:00 in the morning? Say it with me: Undivided attention.
>
> —Olivia Lord

/   /

> It's not a lie...if you believe it.
>
> —Gideon Lord, Keeper of Lies

/ /

> There's a time and place for good deeds: never and nowhere.
>
> —Scarlet Lord,
> Keeper of Nightmares

/ /

> Follow your emotions.
> They'll NEVER lead you astray.
> —Cameo Lord, Keeper of Misery

/ /

> Make sure you take out your troubled past on everyone you encounter today.
>
> —Lazarus the Cruel and Unusual

/   /

> You'll never get a second chance to be the one who threw the first punch.
>
> —Baden, Prince of Hell

/ /

> Don't worry.
> Things can always get worse...
> if you try harder.
>
> —Katarina,
> Royal Hellhound Trainer

/ /

> You can't kill an enemy twice. But you can make him wish he were dead over and over again.
>
> —Taliyah, Future Harpy General

/ /

> Control what you can.
> Let go of what you can't.
> Squeeze something else until it breaks.
>
> —Roc Phaethon,
> Commander of the Astra Planeta

/ /

> Why does the princess always go for the prince?
> Did she even SEE the villain?
> —Neeka the Unwanted

/ /

> Always insist on going twice.
>
> —William the Ever Randy

/ /

> Envy me. I'm perfect.
>
> —Viola, Keeper of Narcissism

/   /

> Go ahead. Take it.
> You deserve it.
>
> —Winter, Keeper of Selfishness

/   /

> Strike first. Ask questions later. Just kidding. Never leave anyone alive to bother questioning.
>
> —Axel, Member of the Elite 7

/ /

- Your bite should always be worse than your bark.
- —Thane, Member of the Elite 7

/ /

> If it's not the worst that could happen, is it even worth doing?
> —Xerxes, The One With Which You Do Not Screw

/ /

> The biggest waste of time? Second chances.
>
> —Tabitha Skyhawk, *Mother Dearest*

/ /

> •Purposely misunderstand everything.•
> Watch the fun unfold.
>
> • —Cameron, Keeper of Obsession •

/ /

> If someone has a sword,
> and you have a sword,
> you should have two swords.
>
> —Puck, Husband to Gillian

/ /

> They don't have to love you.
> But help them remember you.
>
> —Gillian,
> Defender of the Defenseless

/ /

> I'm not saying you should cross any line to win, but I'm not NOT saying you should cross any line to win, either.
>
> —Elin, Dodge Boulder Champion of the World

> The screams of your enemies are the most beautiful lullaby. 5 stars. Highly recommend.
>
> —Koldo, Husband of Nicola

/ /

> If you don't have a dungeon, get one! They're the best!
>
> —Nicola Lane, No Relation to Sunny Sadly

/   /

> Be the worst that could happen to anyone at any given time.
>
> —Bjorn, Member of the Elite 7

/ /

> Be a better killer today than you were yesterday, but not as good as you'll be tomorrow.
>
> —Black, Son of William

/ /

> •Always be thankful for others when they reach their goals.
> Now you've got something to take away from them!
>
> —Green, Son of William

/   /

> Be the architect of your own life. To build, you must first choose your foundation. I went with the blood and bone of my enemies.
>
> —Red, Son of William

/ /

If you're intrigued by these characters and want to read more about them, check out the Lords of the Underworld series. It all begins with *The Darkest Night*...

—Gena Showalter,
Writer of Words,
Destroyer of Reader Dreams,
Healer of Reader Dreams,
Queen of Every World I've Ever Created

/ /

A Small Selection of Books by Gena Showalter

The Lords of the Underworld (Adult Paranormal)
The Darkest Fire (novella)
The Darkest Night
The Darkest Kiss
The Darkest Pleasure
The Darkest Whisper
The Darkest Angel (novella)
The Darkest Prison (novella)
The Darkest Passion
The Darkest Lie
The Darkest Secret
The Darkest Surrender
The Darkest Seduction
The Darkest Craving
The Darkest Touch
The Darkest Torment
The Darkest Promise
The Darkest Warrior
The Darkest Captive (novella)
The Darkest Assassin (novella)
The Darkest King

Gods of War (Adult Paranormal)
Shadow and Ice
Frost and Flame

Tales of an Extraordinary Girl (New Adult Paranormal)
Playing With Fire
Twice As Hot

Young Adult Books

Forest of Good and Evil (Young Adult Fantasy)
The Evil Queen
The Glass Queen

Everlife Series (Young Adult Fantasy)
Firstlife
Lifeblood
Everlife

White Rabbit Chronicles (Young Adult Paranormal)
Alice in Zombieland
Through the Zombie Glass
The Queen of Zombie Hearts
A Mad Zombie Party
Kat in Zombieland (novella)
Down the Rabbit Hole (novella)

Standalones
All Write Already (Non-fiction)
Oh My Goth (Young Adult Paranormal)
Lord of the Vampires (Royal House of Shadows Book 1)

Coming Soon...
Rise of the Warlords (Adult Paranormal)
The Warlord - 2021

Immortal Enemies (Adult Paranormal)
Heartless - 2021

Printed in Great Britain
by Amazon